Contents

Introduction

I want to thank you and congratulate you on downloading this book. In this book, you will find lots of recipes to prepare food in the most delicious and easiest way possible – crockpot dump meals.

Yes, it's as easy as it sounds. All you have to do is to dump all the ingredients into crockpot and after a few hours enjoy delicious meals and only a few recipes require to do something more. This cookbook will offer you a huge collection of mouth-watering dump recipes to choose from, and unlike many cookbooks out there it's well formatted and easy to follow. It's specifically designed for busy people to make it easy to prepare top recipes in much less time.

You will be able to choose from Beef Stroganoff, Chicken Taco Chili, Hungarian Goulash, Cajun Shrimp & Rice and much more. Just look through the table of contents and choose your next dinner. It's that easy... and delicious. Choose now and enjoy!

FREE BONUSES

Every copy of this book comes packed with 2 invaluable bonuses for diabetics and pre-diabetics:

BONUS #1: *Step-By-Step Blueprint **"6 Steps To Reverse Diabetes Naturally And Have A Perfect Health"** - FREE INSTANT DOWNLOAD*
BONUS #2: *Our exclusive newsletter subscription where we share tips, strategies and support to destroy diabetes once and for all - FREE INSTANT ACCESS*

Simply visit the special link below and enter your name & email address to get instant access.

GET INSTANT ACCESS!

WWW.SOURCEOFHEALTHY.COM/6STEPS

Beef Stroganoff

6 servings

INGREDIENTS

- 2 pounds beef chuck roast (sliced into bite-size pieces)
- 1 can or fresh Mushrooms (sliced as desired), optional
- 1 package onion soup mix
- 1 (10 3/4 ounce) can Cream of Mushroom Soup
- 1 (12 ounces) can Ginger Ale
- 2 tablespoon corn starch
- 1 (8 ounces) Sour Cream
- 1 package egg Noodles

DIRECTIONS

1. Place beef chuck roast in the crockpot. Add mushrooms, onion soup mix, cream of mushroom soup, and ginger ale
2. Cook on high for approx. 4-5 hours or low for 6-7 hours, stirring occasionally
3. For the last hour mix 2 tablespoons of cornstarch with a small amount of water and add to thicken. Add sour cream to taste.
4. Cook egg noodles according to package directions
5. Serve stroganoff over noodles and enjoy!

Lazy Man's Pot Roast

8 servings

INGREDIENTS

- 3 pounds chuck roast
- 1 ½ onions, chopped
- 2 garlic cloves, minced
- 1 can (16-ounce) stewed tomatoes
- 1 tablespoon Worcestershire sauce
- 2 tablespoons oil
- coarsely ground pepper, to taste
- flour to cover the roast
- salt, to taste
- 8 ounces water

DIRECTIONS

- Sauté onion and garlic with oil in a pot until transparent.
- Season the roast with salt and pepper and then dredge (lightly) in flour.
- Brown the roast in the pot (on top of the onions and garlic) on both sides for about 10 minutes.
- Transfer roast to the crock pot, add the stewed tomatoes, water, and Worcestershire sauce.
- Cook on setting 4 (of 5) for about 5 hours.
- When done, puree the remaining tomatoes, juices and onions. Return to pan and add thickener for gravy.
- Serve and enjoy!

Secret Ingredient Roast

6 servings

INGREDIENTS

- 4 pound Shoulder Roast
- 1 can Campbell's cream of mushroom soup
- 2 cans Campbell's cream of potato soup
- 2 cups Dr. Pepper
- 1 package Lipton onion soup mix
- ½ – 1 teaspoon seasoning (depending on how spicy you want it)

DIRECTIONS

1. Add all ingredients to crockpot and cook on low for 6-8 hours.
2. Serve and enjoy!

Three Packet Roast

8 servings

INGREDIENTS

- 1 cup water
- 1 packet Italian-style salad dressing mix
- 1 packet ranch dressing mix (regular or buttermilk)
- 1 packet brown gravy mix
- 1 (3 pounds) boneless beef chuck roast

DIRECTIONS

1. In a small bowl, whisk together the water and all 3 packets of seasoning.
2. Place the roast into a sprayed crock pot, and pour the sauce over top.
3. Cook on Low until the roast is easily pierced with a fork, 6 to 8 hours.
4. Serve and enjoy!

General's Chicken

INGREDIENTS

- 4 boneless skinless chicken breasts
- ½ cup water
- 3 tablespoon hoisin sauce
- 2 tablespoon soy sauce
- ½ cup brown sugar
- 3 tablespoon ketchup
- ¼ teaspoon dry ginger
- ½ teaspoon crushed red pepper (more or less to liking)
- 1 tablespoon cornstarch

DIRECTIONS

1. In a mixing bowl, mix together water, hoisin sauce, soy sauce, brown sugar, ketchup, ginger, and crushed red pepper.
2. If you aren't using a liner for your crockpot, spray crockpot with cooking spray and add chicken. Add sauce on top.
3. Cook for 4-6 hours on low. Remove chicken and cut into chunks.
4. Whisk cornstarch in the sauce to thicken it up. If it isn't quite to desired thickness, slowly add more cornstarch teaspoon by teaspoon. But be careful because it can thicken up fast.
5. Add chicken back to the crockpot and allow to heat through for another 15 minutes.
6. Serve over hot rice and garnish with toasted sesame seeds if desired.

Cola Chicken

6 servings

INGREDIENTS

- 4-6 boneless, skinless chicken breasts
- ¼ cup cola
- 1 cup brown sugar
- 2/3 cup white vinegar
- 3 tablespoons minced garlic
- 2 tablespoons soy sauce
- 2 tablespoons corn starch
- 2 tablespoons water
- white rice, cooked

DIRECTIONS

1. Spray the inside of crock pot with non-stick spray. Place chicken in bottom of the insert.
2. In a medium bowl, mix together cola, brown sugar, vinegar, garlic, and soy sauce.
3. Pour over chicken and cook for 6 hours on low or 4 hours on high.
4. Remove chicken from Crockpot and cover tightly with foil.
5. Pour sauce into a small skillet and turn on high heat. In a small bowl, stir together cornstarch and water.
6. Gradually stir in cornstarch mixture into the sauce. Bring to a boil and keep boiling for about 5 minutes until sauce thickens a bit.
7. Remove from heat and allow to cool 5 minutes (sauce will continue to thicken as it cools).
8. Serve chicken over rice with drizzled sauce or in a small bowl for dipping.

Tortellini Lasagne

INGREDIENTS

- 1 pound ground beef
- ½ tablespoon dried, minced onion
- 4 cloves garlic, minced
- 26ounce jar spaghetti sauce
- 1 cup ricotta cheese
- 2 cups fresh spinach
- 19ounce package frozen tortellini
- 1-2 cups shredded mozzarella cheese

DIRECTIONS

1. Brown ground beef in large skillet, drain. Add onion, garlic, and spaghetti sauce. Simmer over medium heat for about 5 minutes, until you really start smelling the garlic. Remove from heat and stir in spinach and ricotta.
2. Spoon 1/3 of the meat sauce on the bottom of crock pot. Top with a ½ package of tortellini. Repeat layers, ending with meat sauce on top. Sprinkle mozzarella.
3. Cook on low 3-4 hours.
4. Serve and enjoy!

Cowboy Casserole

4 servings

INGREDIENTS

- ¼ cup diced onion
- ½ teaspoon pepper
- 1 teaspoon salt
- ½ teaspoon Mrs. Dash
- 1 pound small red potatoes, sliced thin (about 4-5 small red potatoes),
- 1 can of cream of mushroom soup
- 1 pound ground beef browned and drained
- 1 can of diced tomatoes with liquid
- 1 cup canned corn, drained
- 1 can dark red kidney beans, drained
- 1 cup of shredded cheddar cheese

DIRECTIONS

1. Place all of the ingredients except the cheese in a 4- 6-quart crockpot and stir well.
2. Cover and cook on low for 6-7 hours. Uncover crock-pot and sprinkle shredded cheese over top. Re-cover and let cook an additional 30 minutes.
3. Serve and enjoy!

White Bean Chicken Chili

4 servings

INGREDIENTS

- 1.25 pounds Boneless/skinless chicken breast, cut into cubes
- 2 cups Chicken broth
- 1 (11 ounces) Can white corn, drained
- 2 (15 ounce) Cans Great Northern Beans, drained
- 1 Small white onion, chopped
- 1 (4 ounces) Can diced green chilies
- 1 (14 ounces) Can diced tomatoes, drained
- ½ teaspoon garlic powder
- 1 packet White Bean Chili Seasoning Mix
- ½ low-fat Greek yogurt

DIRECTIONS

1. In a blender, puree one can of Great Northern Beans
2. Place all of the ingredients in Crockpot, cover, and cook on low heat for 8 hours.
3. Serve and enjoy!

Chicken Taco Chili

6 servings

INGREDIENTS

- 1 onion, chopped
- 1 (16 ounces) can black beans
- 1 (16 ounces) can kidney beans
- 1 (8 ounces) can tomato sauce
- 1 (14.5 ounces) can corn, drained
- 2 (14.5 ounces) cans diced tomatoes w/chilies
- 1 packet taco seasoning
- 1 tablespoon cumin
- 1 tablespoon chili powder
- 4 boneless skinless chicken breasts

DIRECTIONS

1. Combine all ingredients, except chicken in crock pot. Place chicken on top and cover.
2. Cook on low for 6-8 hours. A half hour before serving, remove chicken and shred. Return chicken to crock pot and stir in.
3. Enjoy!

Mexican Pulled Pork Tacos

6 servings

INGREDIENTS

- 1 pound pork tenderloin
- 1 (15 ounces) can tomato sauce
- 1 tablespoon chili powder
- 1 teaspoon ground cumin
- 1 tablespoon brown sugar
- ½ teaspoon salt
- 3 cloves garlic, minced
- ½ teaspoon cayenne pepper (optional)
- 4 flour tortillas

DIRECTIONS

1. Place pork in the base of your crockpot. In a small bowl, stir together all remaining ingredients, except tortillas. Pour evenly over pork.
2. Cook on low for 6-8 hours.
3. When done, shred the pork using two forks, pulling against the grain of the meat.
4. Serve in warmed tortillas with optional toppings: shredded lettuce, sliced bell peppers, chopped tomatoes, black olives, grated cheddar cheese, and sour cream.

Cajun Shrimp & Rice

6 servings

INGREDIENTS

- 1 pound uncooked shrimp, thawed & peeled
- 2 (14 ounces) cans diced tomatoes, undrained
- 14 ounce can chicken broth
- ¾ cup diced onion
- ¾ cup diced celery
- pepper, to taste
- 6-ounce box Uncle Ben's wild rice mix
- ¼ cup water
- ½ tablespoon Cajun seasonings
- 2 tablespoon minced garlic

DIRECTIONS

1. Combine all ingredients except shrimp and place in a crock pot. Cook on low for 6 hours or high for 3 hours.
2. Meanwhile, cook shrimp in a skillet on medium heat for a few minutes, until they turn pink and opaque.
3. Add cooked shrimp to the crockpot for last 15 min. If cooking on low, turn up the heat to high before adding cooked shrimp for last 15 min. of cooking.
4. Serve and enjoy!

Honey Apple Pork Loin

6 servings

INGREDIENTS

- 2- 2.5 pounds pork loin
- 2 cups apple juice
- red delicious apples, 3 sliced
- 4 tablespoons honey
- cinnamon

DIRECTIONS

1. The night before you want to cook this, use a fork to poke holes in the pork, and then rub the pork with cinnamon. Put apple juice in a Ziploc bag and then put the pork into the marinade. Refrigerate overnight.
2. Lay the apple slices (from two of the apples) in the bottom of the crockpot. Sprinkle with cinnamon.
3. Cut slits in the pork loin (approx. 1 inch). Drizzle some honey into the slits. Then place apple slices from a 3rd apple into the slits.
4. Place the pork loin into the crockpot. Drizzle the top with the remainder of the honey. Place the rest of the apples on top. Sprinkle with cinnamon.
5. Cook on low for 5 hours or until done.
6. Serve and enjoy!

Knock Your Socks off Chicken and Sausage

6 servings

INGREDIENTS

- 1 ½ pounds boneless skinless chicken breasts
- 1 package Andouille sausage (Or you can use smoked sausage, kielbasa, use what you like most)
- 1 (8 ounces) package cream cheese
- 1 cup chicken stock
- ½ cup white wine
- 3 gloves of garlic minced
- 1 small yellow onion diced
- 2 tablespoons grainy mustard
- ½ teaspoon salt
- scallions for garnish
- serve over white rice or buttered noodles

DIRECTIONS

1. In a mixing bowl, whip cream cheese with chicken stock, salt, garlic, mustard and wine until incorporated.
2. Place, chicken and sausage in the bottom of your crock pot. Place onions on top.
3. Pour cream cheese mixture over the top.
4. Cover and place on high for 4 hours or low for 5-6 hours, checking it occasionally to make sure it's not thickening too much. If it is, add more chicken stock or wine.
5. When you are ready to serve, you can place the meal in a baking dish and pop it under the broiler for a couple of minutes for some extra color. (This is optional, but I highly recommend it!)
6. Salt and pepper to taste, serve over rice, quinoa, or pasta.

Russian Apricot Chicken

6 servings

INGREDIENTS

- 1 (12 ounces) jar of apricot preserves
- 1 bottle of Russian salad dressing
- 1 to 2 pounds boneless, skinless chicken breasts
- ½ onion, chopped

DIRECTIONS

1. Place chicken breasts in the crockpot.
2. In a bowl, mix half the jar of apricot preserves with half the bottle of Russian salad dressing. Stir in the chopped onions. Makes sure it's mixed well.
3. Pour the mixture over the chicken.
4. Cook on low for 8 hours.
5. Serve with rice or mashed potatoes.

Ranch Pork Chops

6 servings

INGREDIENTS

- 2 Cans Cream of Chicken soup
- 4-6 Pork Chops
- 1 packet Ranch salad dressing

DIRECTIONS

1. Combine all of the ingredients in the crock pot and cook on high for 4 hours or low for 6-7 hours.
2. Enjoy!

Dump & Run Chicken

6 servings

INGREDIENTS

- 2 stalks celery, rough cut
- 2-3 carrots, rough cut
- 1 onion, rough chopped
- 4-6 boneless skinless chicken breasts
- Seasonings of choice
- 1 can mushroom, drained
- 1 can Campbell's cream of mushroom soup
- 8 red potatoes, scrubbed & sliced in half (optional)

DIRECTIONS

1. Add all of the celery, carrots, and onions on the bottom,1/2 of the seasoned (both sides) chicken, 1/2 of the mushrooms, 1/2 can mushroom soup
2. Repeat layers 2, 3, and 4 (make sure soup is on top)
3. Add potatoes last if using.
4. Cook on low 8-9 hours and enjoy! The chicken is fork tender and the gravy is ample to serve with potatoes or rice!

Lemon & Garlic Chicken

6 servings

INGREDIENTS

- 2 teaspoon minced garlic
- ¼ cup olive oil
- 1 tablespoon parsley flakes
- 2 tablespoons lemon juice
- 4-6 chicken breasts

DIRECTIONS

1. Place all ingredients into a 1-gallon freezer bag. I used wide mouth half gallon Mason jar to hold the bag upright while I filled it with the chicken and other ingredients.
2. After sealing the bag, turn the bag over several times until everything is combined and the chicken is well coated. Freeze flat.
3. Place the frozen chicken in the crockpot and cook on low for 6 to 8 hours.
4. Enjoy!

Hungarian Goulash

6 servings

INGREDIENTS

- 2 pounds beef chuck roast, cut into 1" cubes
- 1 large onion, sliced
- 1 clove garlic, minced
- ½ cup ketchup
- 2 tablespoons Worcestershire sauce
- 1 tablespoon brown sugar
- 2 teaspoons salt
- 2 teaspoons paprika
- ½ teaspoon dry mustard
- 1 cup water
- ½ cup flour

DIRECTIONS

1. Place beef in crock pot, cover with sliced onion.
2. Combine garlic, ketchup, Worcestershire sauce, sugar, salt, paprika, and mustard. Stir in water and pour over meat.
3. Cover and cook on low for 9 to 10 hours.
4. Turn control to high. Dissolve flour in small amount of cold water, stir into meat mixture. Cook on high 10 to 15 minutes or until slightly thickened.
5. Serve goulash over noodles or rice.

American Meatloaf

INGREDIENTS

- 1 ½ pound ground chuck
- 1 egg, beaten
- ¼ cup milk
- 1 ½ teaspoon salt
- 2 slices bread, crumbed
- ½ small onion, chopped
- 2 tablespoons green pepper, chopped
- 2 tablespoons celery, chopped
- 6 potatoes, cut up
- ketchup, to taste

DIRECTIONS

1. Mix egg, milk, salt and breadcrumbs. Let stand to soften.
2. Thoroughly combine egg mixture with meat and chopped vegetables. Shape into a loaf and put in the crockpot. Top with ketchup.
3. Place potatoes around the sides of the loaf (if you peeled them, coat with butter to keep from darkening). Cover and cook on high for 1 hour, then on low for 8-9 hours.
4. Serve and enjoy!

Cheesy Ranch Potatoes

6 servings

INGREDIENTS

- 2 pound small red potatoes quartered
- 1 (8 ounces) package cream cheese, softened
- 1 (10 ¾ ounce) can cream of potato soup
- 1 envelope ranch salad dressing mix
- 1 cup shredded cheddar cheese

DIRECTIONS

1. Place cleaned and quartered potatoes in a 2 quart Crock Pot.
2. In a bowl beat together cream cheese, soup and salad dressing mix. Stir in shredded cheese. Pour over potatoes in crock pot and stir.
3. Cover Crock Pot and Cook on low for 8 hours or until potatoes are tender.
4. Enjoy!

Shredded Beef Tostada

6 servings

INGREDIENTS

- 3 pounds beef roast
- 1 package Campbell's® Crockpot Sauces
- Shredded Beef Taco tostada shells
- shredded lettuce
- fresh salsa
- avocado
- sour cream
- cheese for toppings

DIRECTIONS

1. Place the beef roast, sauces, salsa, avocado, lettuce and sour cream in a crock pot and pour the sauce over it.
2. Cover and cook on low 8 to 12 hours
3. Shred with two forks and serve over tostada shells and top with desired toppings.
4. Serve and enjoy!

Fiesta de Mexico

4 servings

INGREDIENTS

- 1 bag white corn tortilla chips
- 1 pound lean ground beef
- 1 can ranch style beans, undrained
- 3 cups Cheddar cheese, grated
- 1 can cream of mushroom soup
- 1 can cream of chicken soup
- 1 can Ro-Tel tomatoes and chilies
- 2 teaspoons chili powder
- 1/2 cup onion, chopped

DIRECTIONS

1. Spray crock pot with non-stick spray. Strew the bottom with slightly crushed chips.
2. Combine soups, Ro-Tel, chili powder, and onion in a separate bowl and blend well with a whisk.
3. Brown ground beef in a skillet. Drain fat. Add ranch style beans to the beef in the skillet and mix together. (Do not drain the beans).
4. Layer half of the beef mixture over the chips in the crock pot, then half of the soup mixture over the beef, ending with half the cheese over the beef. Repeat these layers once more beginning with chips and ending with cheese. Cook on low for 6-8 hours. Serve and enjoy!

Chicken Santa Fe

5 servings

INGREDIENTS

- 1 (15 ounces) can black beans, rinsed and drained
- 2 (15 ounces) cans whole kernel corn, drained
- 1 cup bottled thick and chunky salsa, divided
- 5 or 6 skinless, boneless chicken breast halves
- 1 cup shredded Cheddar cheese

DIRECTIONS

1. In a crock pot, mix together the beans, corn, and 1/2 cup salsa. Top with the chicken breasts, then pour the remaining 1/2 cup salsa over the chicken. Cover and cook on low for 5-6 hours, or until the chicken is tender and white throughout; do not overcook or the chicken will toughen.
2. Sprinkle cheese on top, cover, and cook until the cheese melts, about 5 minutes.
3. Serve and enjoy!

Gone All Day Casserole

12 servings

INGREDIENTS

- 1 cup uncooked wild rice, rinsed and drained
- 1 cup chopped celery
- 1 cup chopped carrots
- 2 (4 ounces) cans mushroom stems and pieces, drained
- 1 large onion, chopped
- 1 garlic clove, minced
- 1/2 cup slivered almonds
- 3 beef bouillon cubes
- 2 1/2 teaspoons seasoned salt
- 2 pounds boneless round steak, cut into 1-inch cubes
- 3 cups water

DIRECTIONS

1. Place ingredients in a crockpot in the order listed (do not stir). Cover and cook on LOW for 6-8 hours or until rice is tender. Stir before serving.
2. Serve and enjoy!

Fisherman Stew

8 servings

INGREDIENTS

- 28 ounce can crushed tomatoes with juice
- 8 ounce can tomato sauce
- 1 onion, chopped
- 1 cup white wine
- 1/3 cup olive oil
- 3 cloves garlic, minced
- 3 tablespoons parsley
- 1 green pepper, chopped
- 1 hot pepper, chopped
- salt and pepper to taste
- 1 teaspoon thyme
- 2 teaspoon basil
- 1 teaspoon oregano
- 1/2 teaspoon paprika
- 1/2 teaspoon cayenne pepper

Seafood:

- 1 deboned whitefish fillet, cubed
- 1-ounce shrimp
- 1-ounce scallops
- 1-ounce mussels
- 1-ounce clams

- **DIRECTIONS**

1. Place all ingredients except seafood in the crockpot. Cook on low 6 to 8 hours. About 30 minutes before serving, add seafood. Turn crockpot on high and stir gently once or twice.
2. Serve with sourdough bread and enjoy!

Bayou Gumbo

6 servings

INGREDIENTS

- 3 tablespoons all-purpose flour
- 3 tablespoons olive oil
- 1/2 pound smoked sausage, cut into 1/2 inch slices
- 2 cups frozen cut okra
- 1 onion, chopped
- 1 bell pepper, chopped
- 3 cloves garlic, minced
- 1/4 teaspoon red pepper
- 1/4 teaspoon pepper
- 1 14.5 ounces can dice tomatoes, undrained
- 12-ounce package frozen shelled deveined cooked medium shrimp, rinsed
- 1 1/2 cups uncooked regular long-grain white rice
- 3 cups water

DIRECTIONS

1. In a small saucepan, combine flour and oil. Mix well. Cook, stirring constantly, over medium-high heat for 5 minutes. Reduce heat to medium. Cook, stirring constantly, about 10 minutes or until mixture turns reddish brown.
2. Place flour-oil mixture in 3 1/2 to 4-quart crockpot. Stir in all remaining ingredients except shrimp, rice, and water.
3. Cover. Cook on low setting for 7-9 hours,
4. When ready to serve, cook rice in water as directed on package.
5. Meanwhile, add shrimp to gumbo mixture in crock pot. Mix well. Cover. Cook on low setting for additional 20 minutes.
6. Serve gumbo over rice and enjoy.

Easy Salsa Chicken

4 servings

INGREDIENTS

- 4 boneless, skinless chicken breasts
- 2 cups favorite salsa
- salt and pepper

DIRECTIONS

1. Place chicken breasts in a crock pot and cover with salsa. Toss until the chicken is covered.
2. Cover and cook on low for 6-8 hours, or until the chicken shreds easily with a fork.
3. Shred the chicken in the crock pot and toss with the remaining salsa and juices until well-mixed.
4. Serve immediately.

Cajun Shrimp & Rice

6 servings

INGREDIENTS

- 1 pound uncooked shrimp, thawed & peeled
- 2 (14 ounces) cans diced tomatoes, undrained
- 14 ounce can chicken broth
- ¾ cup diced onion
- ¾ cup diced celery
- pepper, to taste
- 6-ounce box Uncle Ben's wild rice mix
- ¼ cup water
- ½ tablespoon Cajun seasonings
- 2 tablespoon minced garlic

DIRECTIONS

1. Combine all ingredients except shrimp and place in a crock pot. Cook on low for 6 hours or high for 3 hours.
2. Meanwhile, cook shrimp in a skillet on medium heat for a few minutes, until they turn pink and opaque.
3. Add cooked shrimp to the crockpot for last 15 min. If cooking on low, turn up the heat to high before adding cooked shrimp for last 15 min. of cooking.
4. Serve and enjoy!

Caribbean Chicken

6 servings

INGREDIENTS

- 2 pounds chicken breasts
- 8 ounce can pineapple chunks with juice
- 1/4 cup packed brown sugar
- 1/2 teaspoon nutmeg
- 1/3 cup orange juice
- 1/2 cup raisins

DIRECTIONS

1. Dump all the ingredients into the crock pot and cook on low for 4-6 hours.
2. Enjoy!

Chicken Cordon Bleu

6 servings

INGREDIENTS

- 5-6 large boneless skinless chicken breasts, cut into pieces
- 1 can of Cream of Chicken Soup
- 1 cup of Milk
- 2 boxes of Chicken Stuffing
- 6 slices of ham
- 6 slices swiss cheese
- 8 tablespoon Butter
- Salt, pepper, garlic powder to taste

DIRECTIONS

1. Place all ingredients (chop chicken with scissors) in the crockpot and cook on low for 6-8 hours.
3. Enjoy!

Turkey Black Bean Chili

6 servings

INGREDIENTS

- 1 pound of ground turkey
- 28 ounce can of tomato sauce
- 2 cans of black beans (15 ounces each), drained and rinsed
- 1 can of petite diced tomatoes (14.5 ounces), undrained
- 1 2/3 cup frozen corn
- 2 large cloves of garlic, minced
- 1 tablespoon paprika
- 1 tablespoon chili powder
- 2 teaspoons ground cumin
- 1 1/2 teaspoon ground oregano
- 1/4 teaspoon crushed red pepper flakes

DIRECTIONS

1. Place all ingredients in crockpot and cook on low for 6-8 hours.
2. Break apart turkey and stir.
3. Serve with shredded cheese and chips!

Chicken Broccoli Alfredo

6 servings

INGREDIENTS

- 4-6 boneless chicken breasts
- 1 (16 ounces) bag frozen broccoli florets
- 2 (16 ounces) jars Alfredo sauce (I use light)
- 1 large green pepper, chopped
- 1 (4 ounces) can sliced mushrooms, drained

DIRECTIONS

1. Place all ingredients in crockpot and cook on low for 4-6 hours.
2. Enjoy!

Thai Peanut Chicken

6 servings

INGREDIENTS

- 4 boneless, skinless chicken breasts
- 1 red pepper, diced
- 1 white onion, chopped
- ½ cup creamy peanut butter
- 1 lime, juiced
- ½ cup vegetable broth
- ¼ cup soy sauce
- ½ tablespoon cumin
- crushed peanuts for topping
- chopped scallions for topping
- cilantro for topping

DIRECTIONS

1. Place all ingredients, except toppings, in crockpot and cook on low for 7-8 hours.
2. Serve over rice.
3. Top with peanuts, scallions, and cilantro.

Savory Pepper Steak

4 servings

INGREDIENTS

- 1½ pounds round steak cut into ½ in strips
- ¼ cup flour
- ½ teaspoon salt
- ½ teaspoon pepper
- 1 small onion, diced
- 4-5 garlic cloves
- 1 green pepper, diced
- 1 red pepper, diced
- 1 (16 ounces) can Italian-style tomatoes
- 1 tablespoon beef bouillon
- 2 tablespoon Worcestershire sauce
- 1 tablespoon steak seasoning
- 1 tablespoon steak sauce

DIRECTIONS

1. Place all ingredients in crockpot and cook on low for 7-8 hours.
2. Enjoy!

Orange Shredded Beef

6 servings

INGREDIENTS

- 1pound boneless beef chuck shoulder roast
- the juice from one navel orange, pulp removed
- the zest from one orange (about 1 tablespoon)
- 2 tablespoons white sugar
- 2 tablespoons rice wine vinegar or apple cider vinegar
- 1 tablespoon soy sauce
- 3 cloves garlic, minced
- 1-inch ginger root peeled and grated (about 1 tablespoon)

DIRECTIONS

1. In a bowl, create sauce: add orange juice, orange zest, sugar, vinegar, soy sauce, garlic, and ginger. Stir to combine.
2. Place all ingredients in crockpot and cook on low for 8-12 hours.
3. Shred meat, mix with remaining sauce in slow cooker, and serve!

Mushroom Barley Stew

4 servings

INGREDIENTS

- 1 pound mushrooms
- 2 sliced carrots
- 1 sliced celery rib
- 1 diced onion
- 15 ounce can diced tomatoes
- 1 cup uncooked barley

DIRECTIONS

1. Place all ingredients in crockpot, add 2 quarts vegetable stock and cook on low for 8 hours.
2. Serve with hot, crusty bread or rolls.

Crock Pot Ribs

6 servings

INGREDIENTS

- 2 pounds of ribs
- 1/2 cup brown sugar
- 1 teaspoon pepper
- 1 Tablespoon garlic powder
- ¾ cup Coke
- 1 Tablespoons honey
- Extra BBQ sauce, optional

DIRECTIONS

1. Place all ingredients in crockpot and cook on low for 8-9 hours.
2. Enjoy!

Beefy Ravioli

6 servings

INGREDIENTS

- 1 pound ground beef, cooked and drained
- 1 (24 ounces) jar spaghetti sauce
- 1 (25 ounces) bag frozen beef ravioli
- 1 cup mozzarella cheese, shredded

DIRECTIONS

1. Cook the ground beef until no longer pink, drain off grease if needed.
2. In a large bowl, open and dump the whole bag of frozen ravioli in it, next add the browned ground beef and the whole jar of spaghetti sauce. Mix well.
3. Place all ingredients in crockpot and cook on low for 6-8 hours.
4. Enjoy!

Pineapple Chicken Burritos

6 servings

INGREDIENTS

- 1½ pounds boneless chicken breast
- ½ (20 ounces) can crushed pineapple, drained
- 1 (15 ounces) cans black beans, rinsed and drained
- 1 cups medium salsa
- 5-6 burrito sized flour tortillas
- 1 (10 ounce) cans green enchilada sauce
- 1 cups shredded cheddar
- 1 cup cooked rice

DIRECTIONS

1. Place all ingredients (except rice) in the crockpot and cook on low for 6-8 hours.
2. Remove the chicken and shred. Mix the chicken back into the crockpot with the rest of the ingredients.
3. Mix in the cooked rice.
4. Fill 5-6 of the burrito tortillas. Place in a 9×13 pan. Pour 1 can of the green enchilada sauce over the burritos.
5. Top with 1 cup of the shredded cheese and place under the broiler on the middle rack until the cheese is nice and melted. About 5 minutes.

Enjoy!

Stuffed Pepper Soup

6 servings

INGREDIENTS

- 1-2 pounds ground beef
- 1 medium onion, chopped
- 2 green peppers, chopped
- 2 15 ounce cans diced tomatoes, undrained
- 1 15 ounce can of tomato sauce
- 1 15 ounce can of water
- 1 can corn
- 1 cup brown rice
- 1 clove garlic
- 1/2 teaspoon parsley
- 1/2 teaspoon oregano
- 2 Tablespoons brown sugar
- 2 teaspoon salt
- 1 1/2 teaspoon pepper

DIRECTIONS

1. Place all ingredients in the crockpot and cook on low for 6-8 hours.
2. Serve with rice.

Cheeseburger Soup

6 servings

INGREDIENTS

- 2 pounds cooked ground beef
- 1 onion, diced
- 1 tablespoon of minced garlic
- 2 cans (14.5 ounce) diced tomatoes
- 1 pound bacon, cooked & broken into pieces
- 6-7 small to medium potatoes, cubed
- 1 cup of chopped or shredded carrots
- 8 ounce package of cream cheese cubed
- 8 cups of chicken broth
- 2 teaspoons of salt
- 1 teaspoon of pepper
- 2 cups of milk
- 1/2 cup of flour
- 3 cups of cheddar cheese, shredded

DIRECTIONS

1. Cook bacon & ground beef. Crumble the bacon & place half of it in a quart freezer bag. Chop the carrots & onion. Chop the cream cheese into cubes.
2. Place all ingredients in the crockpot and cook on low for 6-8 hours.
3. Enjoy!

Conclusion

Thank you for reading. If you want to read my other books you can go to Amazon and check my author page.

If you've enjoyed this book, I would like you to leave a positive review on Amazon. If you want to add something and have some suggestions write them down. I make sure to read each and every review to improve this book.

FREE BONUSES

Every copy of this book comes packed with 2 invaluable bonuses for diabetics and pre-diabetics:

BONUS #1: *Step-By-Step Blueprint **"6 Steps To Reverse Diabetes Naturally And Have A Perfect Health"** - FREE INSTANT DOWNLOAD*
BONUS #2: *Our exclusive newsletter subscription where we share tips, strategies and support to destroy diabetes once and for all - FREE INSTANT ACCESS*
Simply visit the special link below and enter your name & email address to get instant access.

Made in the USA
Columbia, SC
21 September 2020